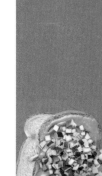

 Published by Ice House Books

Copyright © 2020 Ice House Books
Designed by Smart Design Studio

Ice House Books is an imprint of Half Moon Bay Limited
The Ice House, 124 Walcot Street, Bath, BA1 5BG
www.icehousebooks.co.uk

ISBN 978-1-912867-85-1

Printed in China

DRUNKEN DINING

26 late-night recipes for the intoxicated foodie

ICE HOUSE BOOKS

Photography Credits

CONTENTS

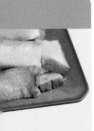

NUGGET *pasta*

WHY THE HELL NOT?!

MAKES: **1 serving**

PREP TIME: **10 minutes**

COOK TIME: **30 minutes**

INGREDIENTS

Handful of spaghetti

Tomato pasta sauce

Chicken or veggie nuggets

Shredded mozzarella cheese

TURN THE PAGE FOR THE METHOD

#1

METHOD

1. Put a pan of water on the hob and cook your pasta *(remember to both light the hob and turn the hob off when you're finished!)*.

2. While you wait for the pasta to cook, pop the oven on and dance around the kitchen.

3. Once it's cooked, drain the spaghetti and put it back in the pan. Pour over the tomato sauce and give everything a stir, then put it all in your baking dish. Add a layer of chicken nuggets on top and the mozzarella.

4. Try not to fall asleep while you cook your nugget pasta for 15 minutes *(we recommend setting a timer)*.

   Serve OR enjoy straight out of the baking dish!

DIFFICULTY RATING

FIRE EXTINGUISHER RATING **3**

CHEESE-PUFF *cereal*

FOR THOSE EVENINGS WHEN YOU STUMBLE HOME AND FANCY CEREAL, BUT THEN REALISE YOU'VE RUN OUT...

METHOD

MAKES: **a weird meal**

PREP TIME: **30 seconds**

1. Grab a bowl, tip in your cheese puffs and pour over some milk *(or just add the milk to the crisp packet if you're past the bowl stage of the night).*

INGREDIENTS

- 1 packet cheese puffs
- Milk

DIFFICULTY RATING

FIRE EXTINGUISHER RATING **0**

#2

THE weggle

ONE POTATO WAFFLE, ONE EGG.
WHAT DO YOU GET? A WEGGLE!

MAKES: 1 serving

PREP TIME: 5 minutes

COOK TIME: 5–10 minutes

INGREDIENTS

- Sunflower oil
- 1 frozen potato waffle
- 1 free-range egg
- 1 soft white roll
- Ketchup

METHOD

1. Dig out your frying pan and add a little bit of oil (not the whole bottle). Pop the pan on the hob.

2. Add a waffle to the pan and fry it on one side until it's a nice golden colour – if you smell burning, you've left it too long.

3. Flip the waffle over and crack an egg on top – one handed like a chef if you dare – and let the egg trickle into the waffle holes. Leave until the egg is cooked.

4. Transfer your Weggle into a soft, white roll, with an extra waffle for good measure if you fancy, and garnish with ketchup. Done!

FIRE EXTINGUISHER RATING 3

DIFFICULTY RATING

#3

BARBECUE *rice*

A SIMPLE WAY TO GET A PUNCH OF FLAVOUR WHEN HAND-EYE COORDINATION IS LACKING.

MAKES: 1 serving

PREP TIME: 2 minutes

INGREDIENTS

- 1 pouch of microwavable rice
- Barbecue sauce

METHOD

1. Pop the pouch of rice in the microwave and watch it whizz around for a couple minutes.

2. Steam your face and try not to burn your fingers as you release the rice from the evil hot pouch into a bowl. Squeeze on your barbecue sauce and tuck in!

FIRE EXTINGUISHER RATING 1

DIFFICULTY RATING

#4

NACHOS IN A *mug*

#5

BECAUSE FOOD IN A MUG IS #GOALS.

MAKES: 4 mugs
(breakfast is covered then)

PREP TIME: 5 minutes

COOK TIME: 5 minutes

INGREDIENTS

- Salsa
- Tin of black beans, drained
- 4 handfuls of tortilla chips
- Black olives, sliced
- Grated cheddar cheese
- Sour cream

DIFFICULTY RATING

FIRE EXTINGUISHER RATING 3

METHOD

1. Mix the salsa and beans together without mashing the beans *(or decorating the walls)*.

2. Spoon your salsa and bean mix into each mug then add a handful of tortilla chips. Top off with sliced black olives and cheeeeeese!

3. Pop the mugs, one at a time, into the microwave and count to 60 *(while singing better than you've ever sung before)*.

4. Top each nacho mug with sour cream if it takes your fancy, and indulge!

KETCHUP *pasta*

WHEN YOU DON'T HAVE PASTA SAUCE, TOMATO KETCHUP WILL DO THE TRICK.

MAKES: **1 serving**

PREP TIME: **5 minutes**

COOK TIME: **10 minutes**

INGREDIENTS

- Handful of spaghetti
- Tomato ketchup

METHOD

1. Cook your pasta in a pan of water on the hob.

2. Once it's cooked, drain the spaghetti and plonk it on a plate, then go crazy with your ketchup.

DIFFICULTY RATING

FIRE EXTINGUISHER RATING **3**

FISH FINGER
sandwich

AN ABSOLUTE BEAST OF A CLASSIC!

MAKES: 1 sandwich

PREP TIME: 5 minutes

COOK TIME: 15 minutes

INGREDIENTS

- 3 slices of bread
- All the fish fingers
- Tomato ketchup

FIRE EXTINGUISHER RATING 1

METHOD

1. Whack the oven on and cook the fish fingers for 15 minutes – about the same amount of time it takes you to watch half a cartoon comedy *(with one eye open)*.

2. Once they're cooked, layer them between the slices of bread and top with ketchup to create the ultimate sandwich.

#7

PIZZA *chips*

THIS **PHENOMENON** CHANGES EVERYTHING.

MAKES: **4 servings**

PREP TIME: **5 minutes**

COOK TIME: **15–20 minutes**

INGREDIENTS

- Chips (obvs)
- Tomato pizza sauce
- Shredded mozzarella cheese
- Sliced pepperoni

FIRE EXTINGUISHER RATING **2**

DIFFICULTY RATING

METHOD

1. Put the oven on, fill a tray with chips and pop them in.

2. Repeat instruction number 1, having not actually turned the oven on/put the chips in the first time.

3. Once the chips are cooked, tip them into a baking dish without getting them all on the floor. Pour over the pizza sauce and add all the cheese and pepperoni. Put the dish in the oven.

4. Watch the oven like your life depends on it and bake until the cheese has melted. Garnish if you're feeling fancy and enjoy the cheese oozy-ness!

#8

CHEESE *toastie*

EVERYBODY'S BEST DRUNKEN FRIEND.

MAKES: **2 toasties (because when has one ever been enough?)**

PREP TIME: **5–10 minutes**

COOK TIME: **10 minutes**

INGREDIENTS

- 4 slices of bread
- Butter
- Cheese slices

FIRE EXTINGUISHER RATING **2**

METHOD

1. Pull out your frying pan and put it on the hob.

2. Butter one side of each slice of bread. It's a tricky business remembering which side you buttered, but put a slice in the pan, butter-side-down, add a slice of cheese (or slices if you're feeling cheeky) and top off with another slice of bread, butter-side-up.

3. Cook the toastie for a couple minutes *(you've left it too long if the kitchen smells of burning)*, flip it over and cook the other side *(if you can be bothered)*. Do the same for the second toastie if you haven't already eaten it as a sandwich while waiting for the toastie to cook.

4. EAT!

#9

PEANUT BUTTER
&pickle sandwich

THE STRANGEST OF DELICACIES
BUT DELICIOUS TO SOME...

MAKES: **1 sandwich**

PREP TIME: **2 minutes**

INGREDIENTS

- 2 slices of bread
- Peanut butter
- Pickles

METHOD

1. Slather some peanut butter onto your bread and layer the pickles on one slice. Sandwich it together and slice it into triangles *(because that's the best way to eat a sandwich).*

BON APPÉTIT!

FIRE EXTINGUISHER RATING **1**

DIFFICULTY RATING

#10

PESTO *pasta*

THE ULTIMATE COMFORT FOOD, AND YOU CAN EAT IT STRAIGHT OUT OF THE PAN!

MAKES: **1 serving**

PREP TIME: **5 minutes**

COOK TIME: **10 minutes**

INGREDIENTS

- Handful of farfalle pasta (or whatever you have in the cupboard)
- Green pesto
- Grated Parmesan
- Leafy things to make it look gourmet

METHOD

1. Put a pan of water on the hob and cook your pasta. You might want to keep at least one eye on the pan in case the water boils over …

2. When it's cooked, drain the pasta then put it back in the pan. Spoon in the green pesto and mix it in.

3. Sprinkle over some Parmesan, then garnish your pan of pasta if you have anything resembling an edible green leaf.

TUCK IN!

FIRE EXTINGUISHER RATING **2**

DIFFICULTY RATING

#11

PIZZA *sandwich*

NAME A BETTER
SANDWICH FILLING -
I DARE YOU.

METHOD

MAKES: everything you've ever wanted

PREP TIME: 5 minutes

COOK TIME: 10–12 minutes

INGREDIENTS

- Pizza of choice
- Sliced bread

1. Pop the oven on. Don't panic when the light goes out, it's just time to slide your pizza in.

2. Sit on the kitchen floor and scroll through Instagram while you wait for the pizza to cook, about 10–12 minutes. When it's cooked, slice it up.

3. Get out your bread and put a slice of pizza between two pieces of bread. **Shower with sauces or enjoy as is!**

FIRE EXTINGUISHER
RATING **2**

DIFFICULTY RATING

#12

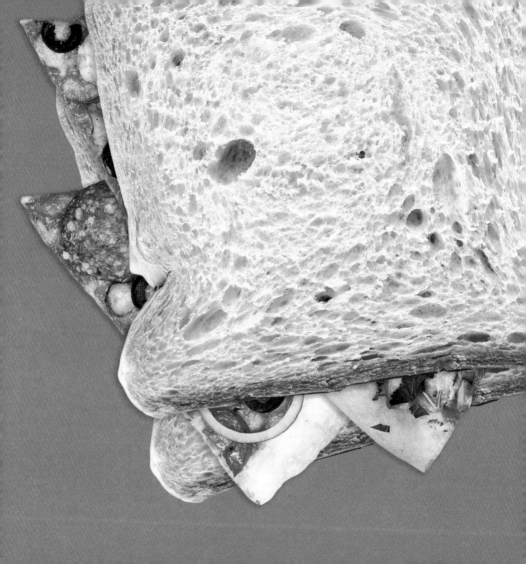

POPCORN *with*
ketchup

MAKES: **several servings**
but let's be honest, we're not sharing

COOK TIME: **2 minutes**

INGREDIENTS

- 1 pack of salted popcorn
- Ketchup

METHOD

1. Microwave the popcorn and try not to cause an explosion.

2. Put the popcorn in a big-ass bowl and create a piece of ketchup art on top. DIVE IN!

DIFFICULTY RATING

FIRE EXTINGUISHER RATING **1**

#13

Scrambled eggs
WITH JAM

BECAUSE WHAT ELSE ARE YOU GONNA HAVE WITH YOUR SCRAMBLED EGGS...?

MAKES: 1 serving

COOK TIME: depends on how you like your eggs

INGREDIENTS

- Free-range egg(s)
- Milk
- Jam

FIRE EXTINGUISHER RATING 1

DIFFICULTY RATING

#14

METHOD

1. Nobody's got time for a frying pan when you can microwave your eggs instead. Find a microwave-safe bowl, crack in your eggs and add a little bit of milk and some salt and pepper if you're feeling fancy. Give it all a mix.

2. Pop the bowl in the microwave, whack it on high and count to 45 seconds. Take it out and give the eggs a quick stir, then pop them in again and count to 30.

3. Find yourself some jam and and add a spoonful *(or two!)* to your eggs. TUCK IN!

PEANUT BUTTER
& *onion sandwich*

WHY SHOULD ONION BE SAVED ONLY FOR CHEESE?
PB & O IS THE NEW BLACK.

MAKES: the weirdest/most delicious food combo

PREP TIME: 5 minutes

INGREDIENTS

- 2 slices of bread
- Peanut butter
- Onion (as much as you can handle raw)

METHOD

1. Spread the peanut butter on your bread.

2. Chop up that onion like a chef and scatter it on one slice. Sandwich with the other slice of bread, cut it into triangles and enjoy!

DIFFICULTY RATING

FIRE EXTINGUISHER RATING 1

#15

French Fries
WITH HONEY

IT'S IMPOSSIBLE TO EAT FRIES WITHOUT DIP BUT WHAT DO YOU DO WHEN YOU'VE RUN OUT?

MAKES: 1 serving (unless you're going all out and buying more than one side of fries)

PREP TIME: 20 seconds

INGREDIENTS

- Takeaway French fries
- Honey

FIRE EXTINGUISHER RATING 1

DIFFICULTY RATING

METHOD

1. Try not to be too lairy as you queue for your French fries – you don't want to be chucked out.

2. When you get home, find the honey you forgot you had in the back of the cupboard, pour it all over your fries, and enjoy!

OBVS THIS RECIPE ONLY REALLY WORKS IF YOU DON'T
EAT ALL THE FRIES BEFORE YOU GET HOME...

PICKLES
& ice cream

FOR WHEN DRUNKEN CRAVINGS MIRROR
PREGNANCY ONES...

MAKES: the strangest dessert ever

PREP TIME: 1 minute

METHOD

1. Scoop as much ice cream as will please your heart into a bowl, and instead of topping it off with a sugary sauce or sprinkles, decorate it with slices of pickles!

INGREDIENTS

- Ice cream
- Pickles

FIRE EXTINGUISHER RATING **0**

#17

JELLY BEAN *omelette*

SOMETIMES, IT TAKES BEING DRUNK TO BE DARING...

MAKES: **1 omelette**

PREP TIME: **5 minutes**

COOK TIME: **5 minutes**

INGREDIENTS

- 2 free-range eggs
- Li'l bit of butter
- Handful of jelly beans

FIRE EXTINGUISHER RATING **2**

DIFFICULTY RATING

METHOD

1. Whisk the eggs together like you're creating a new dance move.

2. Heat the butter in a frying pan and don't freak when it starts to foam – that's meant to happen. Now's the time to pour in your whisked eggs and watch the magic happen.

3. Gently push the edges away from the sides of the pan as they start to set – without turning your omelette into scrambled eggs – and give the pan a shake *(flip if you're feeling ambitious)*.

4. Add the jelly beans, fold the omelette in half, and try to elegantly slide it onto a plate – again, trying not to turn it into scrambled eggs.

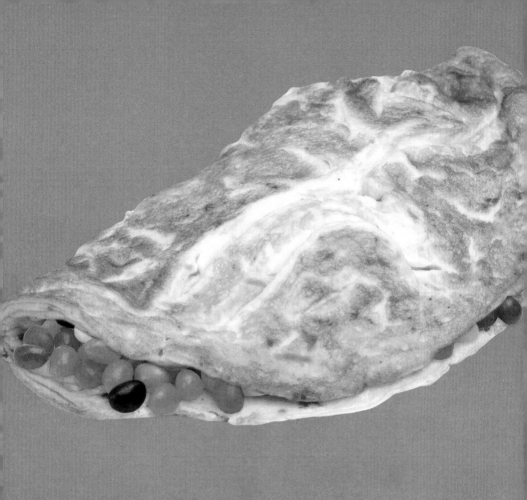

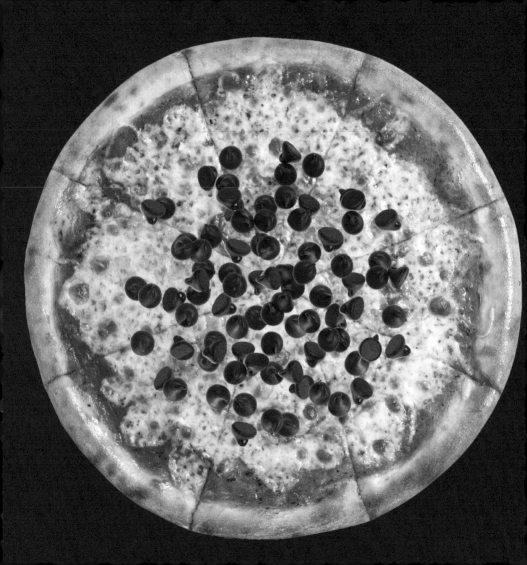

Pizza WITH
MELTED CHOCOLATE

DON'T BE FOOLED. THIS ISN'T A DESSERT PIZZA. OH NO...

METHOD

MAKES: 1 pizza

PREP TIME: 5 minutes

COOK TIME: 10–12 minutes

INGREDIENTS

- 1 pizza of your choice
- Chocolate chips

FIRE EXTINGUISHER RATING 2

DIFFICULTY RATING

1. Pop the oven on and let it warm up all toasty like.

2. Take your pizza out of the wrapping because no one needs plastic in their food, and decorate it with your chocolate chips.

3. Put the pizza *(the right way up)* in the oven and watch the chocolate melt into the cheeeese! When it's cooked, slice it up or just tear chunks off.

#19

AVOCADO &
peanut butter toast

WHEN YOU HAVE THE
MUNCHIES YOU HAVE
TO ENJOY WHATEVER'S
TO HAND...

MAKES: **1 serving**

PREP TIME: **5 minutes**

INGREDIENTS

- An avocado
- 2 slices of bread
- Peanut butter

FIRE EXTINGUISHER
RATING **1**

METHOD

1. Take a moment to pray that your avocado won't be (a) hard as rock, or (b) rotten to the core.

2. Use your avocado ninja skills to break that thing open and slice it *(without severing hands and/or fingers)*.

3. Toast your bread and spread on the peanut butter, top with the avocado slices and enjoy!

#20

TORTILLA CHIPS
& *chocolate spread*
sandwich

WE ALL KNOW CHOCOLATE AND TORTILLA CHIPS ARE A GREAT COMBO, SO WHY NOT TURN IT INTO A SANDWICH?

MAKES: **1 sweet 'n' salty sandwich**

PREP TIME: **5 minutes**

INGREDIENTS

- Sliced bread
- Chocolate spread
- Tortilla chips

FIRE EXTINGUISHER RATING **0**

DIFFICULTY RATING

METHOD

1. Decorate the bread slices with your tortilla chip and chocolate combo. You could smear the chocolate spread on the bread like butter, or squeeze it over the tortilla chips if it comes in a squeezy tube. However you do it, own it and enjoy your masterpiece.

OLIVE OIL
&ice cream

DON'T BE FOOLED, THIS COMBINATION IS A **TRUE DELICACY!** LOOK IT UP IF YOU DON'T BELIEVE US...

MAKES: 1 serving

PREP TIME: 1 minute

INGREDIENTS

- Ice cream
- Olive oil

METHOD

1. Scoop some ice cream into a bowl and ditch the chocolate sauce. Instead drizzle over a helping of olive oil.

DIFFICULTY RATING

FIRE EXTINGUISHER RATING 0

#22

CHOCOLATE BISCUITS
with *orange juice*

FORGET ABOUT DUNKING YOUR BISCUITS IN TEA...
IT'S ALL ABOUT ORANGE JUICE NOW! ADD A TANG TO
YOUR SNACK AND LET THE CREAM SOAK UP THE JUICES.

MAKES: for a very happy bunny

PREP TIME: 20 seconds

METHOD

1. Pour yourself a glass of orange juice, grab your Oreos®, tuck yourself into bed and dunk those bad boys in your glass of Vitamin C!

INGREDIENTS

- Packet of Oreos® (because who has the willpower to only eat a few?!)
- Glass of orange juice

FIRE EXTINGUISHER RATING **0**

DIFFICULTY RATING

#23

BUTTER & SUGAR *toast*

BECAUSE SUGAR WORKS WITH EVERYTHING. RIGHT?!

MAKES: a very sweet treat

INGREDIENTS

- Sliced bread
- Butter
- Sugar

METHOD

1. Toast your bread and try not to doze off while you wait for it to ping back up.

2. Go crazy with the butter and sprinkle over as much sugar as you can handle.

NOM!

FIRE EXTINGUISHER RATING 1

#24

RICE - PUFF
cereal treat

MAKES: **1 serving**

PREP TIME: **1 minute**

COOK TIME: **1 minute**

INGREDIENTS

- Smidgen of unsalted butter
- 4 large marshmallows
- Rice Krispies®

DIFFICULTY RATING

FIRE EXTINGUISHER RATING **1**

#25

METHOD

1. Firstly, make sure you're using a deep-ish, microwaveable bowl – killing the microwave isn't the way you want to end the night with a bang.

2. Put a tiny bit of butter in the bowl and microwave it until melted. Add the marshmallows and microwave again, counting to 20.

3. Take the bowl out of the microwave, mix the butter and marshmallows then stir in the Rice Krispies® until they're coated.

DIG IN!

ICE CREAM
sandwich

FOR WHEN YOU CAN'T DECIDE
IF YOU FANCY SWEET OR SAVOURY...

MAKES: **1 sandwich**

PREP TIME: **5 minutes**

INGREDIENTS

- Bread roll
- Ice cream
- All of the sprinkles

METHOD

1. Carefully half your bread roll *(without amputating a finger)* and fill it with your favourite flavoured ice cream *(or whatever's available)*.

2. Get creative with your sprinkles and, well, sprinkle them over the ice cream.

TUCK IN!

FIRE EXTINGUISHER
RATING **0**

DIFFICULTY RATING

#26